Before the Epiphany

Alice Shantel Saunders

ISBN 10: 061589075X

ISBN 13: 978-0615890753

TL Publishing Group LLC

PO Box 151073

Tampa, FL 33684

www.tlpublishing.org

Table of Contents

Acknowledgements

The fruit of labor is so sweet. I give praise and thanks to my Lord and Savior Jesus Christ for continually blessing me. His unwavering grace brought me this far. Jesus kept me. He will do the same for you.

My family and friends, thank you for your continued love, prayers, and support.

To my Torridian family around the world: thank you. This is for you.

Confessions:

The Good, the Bad, & the Ugly

Poetic Interlude: Art Collection

My head hurts
Literally

I normally don't go this deep
Nonetheless here I am
With this pen
Releasing tears
That I'm tired of drowning in

This recent suppression has kept me submerged and in a cage
And I'm no Houdini nevertheless
Watch me try and escape
So yes I'm making my struggles known

I'm tired of my fears being critically acclaimed
By the other emotions I've failed to tame
So this is not a time for me to stand here and act mundane
Or blend in with the shame

This platform is steep
So I'm sliding like its oblique

Sometimes when I'm relating a poem
I wish I could say that it wasn't real
Or at least that it wasn't about me however
As of late these poems are as real as

The emotional handicap I've developed
From all of the pitfalls
I didn't correctly rebound from
Or the broken pieces of me I didn't realign right

So I'm sitting here letting tears from this pen
Stain this paper
Because I need to conjugate
This numbness – sort it all out

Yet and still it's a shame the way these lines
Are nothing other than false fiction
I can't do anything except place fines

On my heart for allowing the friction

To run me in the wrong direction
I let worry turn this introspection
Sour so I guess you can call this recollection
The unveiling of my emotional art collection

Diseased Pleas

The heart weighs heavy
When the world acts like a levy
Continually relentless in its compressions
Seeking to inject postmortem dimensions
Of why one hasn't conformed to
The status quo that's really rue

I'm so sick of smiles and rings
That belong to cryptic affairs that bare strings
I've been in this soup line
Waiting too for my assignment
My arm was out stretched
Bowl in hand – why must it be so far-fetched
That I too am waiting on my fair share

Then the world slapped my hand as if to demean my prayer
As others rushed passed their eager feet
Were taunts to my heart that still beats during this deceit

I'm a raw egg with only one weak shell
So an encounter leads to cracks that raise hell
Because of the spillage that follows which
Is why I'm here out of my niche
Stuck trying to gather pieces that
Won't hold during this debate that fails to adjust
To crescent needs that plead for an end to this season
That bleeds nothing but treason

Assaulted Truths

A silence deafening to the ears
Speaks in volumes to scandalized lips and
A fearful narcissism suffers as it saunters amongst sentient eyes
While humility lies upon a foreign yet damaged tongue

A treacherous conscious spreads its contagion
Slowly but painfully infecting, affecting, effecting at each sludgy pace
Stuck in a vain aspect
Ascending in a downward cycle

Subrogation is not waived at this juncture
Oh "lucidity" you say? Try the next light
Because the reflection cast back at this stop
Is a perception of many and none of the façade induced self

A voice of one brought down the society of many
Truths lie hidden and covered in dust
Next to skeletons that can't see the light
For the darkness that surrounds them
So they lie in wait – paid in full

Flirting with the knowledge that Time is a harlot
Rightfully screwing everyone for a price
As premature notions take the forefront of a concocted reality
And head a battle with only one known end in sight

Who shall be sacrificed first?
The luscious taste of death
Falls upon an already decayed liaison
No known repentance or countenance in sight resides here

Caught up in the misconception that
Infuriating actions can breed peace through justification
Instead what is now is not what was but
What was never was what it was

This weakened humanity is gathering its pieces
Unsure of how to start the end
Temporary or not is not a matter
As Time fails to erase words

Whereas distance from such only ceases the festering of wounds
A scar will always remain
A disfigured reminder of the capabilities of an unsettled ache
That assaults the psyche

Because one sided truths take claim of a nonexistent space
The rise and fall of an episodic tradition sees its demise
And Tomorrow has promised a healing
Of Yesterday's injuries

For whom partake?

Dream

I dreamed about you last night
Even though you're already gone
Memories of you
Vibrate throughout my heart
Putting my entire vibe
On an irregular rhythm

You left your mark
So now I'm left with a hollow
Indentation of you
At times sleep is a pleasure
While at other times
It's a painful reminder

Of what I must live without
I remember the strain of
Promises made
And I regret the ones
I didn't keep
No wonder in the end

Our love was traced with
Ligature marks
That resembled the
Trifling relations
We willfully submerged ourselves in
Maybe we were right but

Time was trite
Or maybe you were right
And I was a fool
To try and act like your love was a tool
Either way I don't want to keep
These dreams at bay
I'll let them have their way
If it means subduing my dismay

You and Me

You and me
One of us is heaven
And the other is hell
The difference being
The moment of purgatory in between
Where we call ourselves a couple

So you and me
We're not the sun and moon
You don't awake my senses
And I no longer illuminate your world
So we can't coexist in the same atmospheric conditions
Let alone the same solar system

So how are you going to
Tell me I'm your air
You should be on fire because of the friction
The constant way your words
Contrast with your actions

Catatonic Pleasantries

Mountains crumble
Trees die
Seasons exist
So why are we fighting?

We're becoming tectonic plates
Letting what's inside build up
We start with tremors
Because of the friction
That sent unheeded warnings
Until the big quake came and the fault lines were too big to ignore

Then volcanos formed

When you erupt
I can't get away from you fast enough
The devastation is unbearable
This is more of a confession
Than it is a rant

I loved you religiously…
I never broke the term down
However looking back at it now
You were my habit
My bad habit
One that I was maintaining
Because I was insistent that I could turn your
Volcanos into a beautiful landscape
But the lava that is your mentality
Was too hot to trudge through

I could deal with the mountains and valleys
But the scorching river
Was a threat to the state
Of my emotions

I had every structure set up perfectly
I couldn't take that risk anymore

So I'd tell you I love you

However if I let honesty have its way
I'd have to say that
I can't stay and live
With this covert dismay

I need to lay waste
To all of this haste
That has me disgraced
Due to the contamination
Of this romantic toxic waste

The Ties that Bind

I've lived a thousand lives
And during each divide
I could not find a love line quite like yours
To make my centerline

So be it far from me
To submit unto you
Love lies that break the ties
That bind this quintessential design

The weight of your heart
Is what broke the mold
Like it was foretold
I could no more withhold
My love then I could assault my own heart
Which you now hold

I wake up lying next to
The hero who subdued my dreams
So lay your love upon me
Separate dreams and make reality like
The sweet fiction that feeds these daylight fantasies of mine
You mastered with ease the extremes
So the cross-over was more than an appease

You were the storm that
Rocked the proverbial boat of
'What-wasn't-being-said' concepts
So the affections are no longer clandestine

I can touch you now
And know I'm not going to wake up
In the middle of the night
Like a feign looking for a hit

You provoke thoughts and beckon epiphanies

You're my dream and my reality
My sun and moon
The trade off in your personality

Is an added bonus
So when you go from
Night to day
Or day to night
It doesn't matter
The degree
Or variable

We're burning bridges
The way we were always meant to
Because of the ties that bind us

Gravitational Seduction

Our matings have become so dynamic
You perfected the art of defense-structured relations
Not permitting any off color abstract to detour us
From our balance

You said you loved me
What my heart took in was
The affirmation of latent desires
What took us so long?

You're the element that perfected paramount liaisons
We haughtily inhaled the love
Each of us had to give
Individually receiving more than our fair share

It's to our own benefit we love and live in abundance
I should tell you
Like a purebred addict
All it took was that initial sample

Branded I was yours

The sweet aroma of passion that was all you
Completely overloaded my senses
You captivated my desire
Causing it to humble to the will of your love

So now, we're caught in this
Gravitational seduction
Melting into a solid
Single representation of us
Where I can humbly
Trace pieces of me
And find the remains of you

Dejected

Long before we could get an efficient start
You emotionally left so
We began to wither
Like a flower that prematurely
Reached the end of its peak

Brought about by lawless desires
Pieces of me flaked off you
Like I was a season

So as our love died
Like a badly lit flame
My heart went through withdrawal
At the same time my psyche
Was attacked by memory cloaked sensations
These tremors had my entire thought process
Appended

Gone was the ecstasy
That left us inebriated
Here and now is
The ill-fated residue
That leaves our souls
Emotionally defunct
Set apart from
The beauty that
Was once known as us

You didn't have anything to say
Save the silence the spread propaganda
Across the union of our love
I loved you with a passionate pride that
Embellished in the feeling
Now I simply tire of the emotion
That seeps from my heart and forms these tears

The loss of
Individualistic desires was supposed to
Be a beneficial factor in the attainment of us
Yet

Somehow realities turned out to be veneer induced fantasies

Not in line with destiny's scale
So the balance was off
Instead of completing each other
We ended up depleting one another

Benched

If she held my breath at "Hello"
Then she mercilessly seized my heart at "Goodbye"
Taking measurable pieces of me with her
I can't come to myself without her

She's the opportunistic measure
That carried a seductive risk
She had me ready to strike against myself for believing
Systematic normalcy could be purposed with her

Our passions mirror the desires
Of each other
Reflecting the aspirations long since
Conditioned to the romantic vibe of the other

She's the relapse that soothes the angst that surfaces when she's not
near.

The moment she walked out
My soul became in excess of the drought
That pilfered any remaining sense of reasonable doubt
That maybe it wasn't me

Yet at this juncture
I can't even fool myself
The foul admittance
Would be a hindrance to the profitable desires
My soul wishes to claim

I've been benched

Never - Part I

I never should have let her go
I should have held on tighter
Despite the fact that
My passion was losing its grip
On the realty of the matter

I missed the moment it happened
The point in time
When she emotionally left
Pilfering any common sense
That remained on my behalf
I suppose that's why
I acted like I did

My heart was straining
To hold onto the pieces that
She left behind

It should have been her
My whole system is fractured
Like a picture puzzle
It was the pieces of her
That made the overall
View complete
And something to behold

Never - Part II

Always
I thought it was him
Distilling my desires
Into the purest of forms

The view was great from afar
But time, the subtle nuisance
That it is
Wore away at the façade
And showcased the
Disproportionate elegancies
That marked our sincerities

No one told me about
The factors excluded from
Love's view
Nor was it related to me there would be
Pains that accompanied that knowledge

Now I'm here with a heart
That's deformed
At an age that's unfortunately informed

I never should have went in the way I did
Acting like love would build over time
Without setting up any initial foundation
No wonder my love quickly ran dry
Now I'm roughed up around the edges
With any form of friction tearing at my senses and
Deconstructing my stability

Insanity

Dreams stood still
While time had its way

Details ended up marking us like perforations
Intent on keeping us far from united yet not truly apart

Each attempt at a replay wore
Away at us like too many washes on the wrong cycle

I remember how the screams kept tempo and ran
Parallel with the mutual
Tears that were followed by assassinated dreams

We failed
Failed at starting
Maintaining
Growing
And especially at ending

Yet we continually tried to repeat us
Each time hoping a different version of us was relayed.
Not realizing this "backseat" concept
Only cemented our fate

The Currency of Tears

What if I grabbed a fistful of my tears
And rolled them like dice
Tell me what would the odds be that you'd still stay
If I gambled it all and let my heart spill

Because what's hiding behind this dam
Is as dangerous as the fears
That infect my concentration but I'm addicted
To the risk
Even if the odds are stacked against me
I still find myself contributing to this
Hole we've both been digging

Tell me
Is there a gamblers anonymous for lovers
That just don't know when to call it quits
Because I can't find a measure of hope
To hold onto long enough to keep me
Sane while I constantly keep
Turning blind eyes to the obvious

I've been investing in a fool's luck
Hoping to find wisdom in
Thoughts that lead me to these dead ends
Where I'm left with nothing but a pocket full of tears

You Give Me Butterflies

I hate that you give me butterflies

As soon as I think I'm over you
You come back around
And throw my fragile world off its axis

It hurts a bit more
Each tear is a bit heavier
Each scream is more frightening
Yet and still my grip is firm
Because I'm trying to dream my way through this
And bypass reality
But how do I give you the blueprint to my heart?

Haven't I been down this road before
Singing this tired old song?

Before I let you go this time
Let me love you a 'lil bit longer
Because I promise I won't break
These cracks you see over my heart
Form a hunter's mark
Because I was prey to a love that I wasn't ready for

Give me a chance
To imprint upon you my need for closure
Then you'll understand why I'm stuck
In this same scene

And if I could rid myself of these butterflies
Then maybe it'd be easier
To avoid reliving memories that
Deepen the dents in my heart

Developing into Alice:

Growing Pains Included

Lyrical Storm

Second light is a nuisance that maintains
These rigid subconscious chains
So I might as well pick up this pen
That opens up the gambling den
I don't know what's going to come from
This flood once I let the ink from my pen become
The natural disaster with the storm category unknown
Until it becomes time for me to assess and atone
For the damage done
So due to the delayed aid I've begun
Looting from the crevices of my own mind
Searching for understanding and allowing biases to create an
abnormality
Throughout the results
So my consults tend to mirror insults
Yet though my fractured goodwill
Is skewed I'm still determined to drill
And let this spill erupt
So I'll let my later response come through abrupt
Like a mock apology because
It's too late for sincerity and 'cause
Let's face it I truly don't give a damn
Who gets caught when the dam
Collapses because the backdrop
Needs to be cleaned of this failed crop
That's stealing my props
In hopes that this flow drops
But the question isn't "when
Will the season end?"
But what category storm am I in?

Dripping Red

If we must die
Let it not be like
Prisoners of an inapt cause
Socially chained and economically gagged
By and through the greed of fixtures and transports
In an attempt to pacify a match waiting for friction

No longer will our words be muffled
Due to a lack of stimulation

They may call the death of this flesh
A casualty of war
But we will turn fleshless voices into warriors
Where proverbial legends are built
Around the battles we initiate, conquer, and win

So if we must die
Let it be in the red water
Where others can't cling to
This semblance of penance
Where desires asphyxiate and
Courage rises to the surface

Come!
Others will gather and watch
In an attempt to decipher
How we cripple the enemy
Without shifting our eyes

So when we die
Bury us with the politically incorrect regime
That stands proud of being perfectly abstract
Where our battle cry is our epitaph and
Our elegy is the school lesson
For young academic warriors to follow

Because they must not be like
Insurgent robots slave to a socialistic hell
We must die and show them heaven

Lines

There is a thin line
In between yesterday and tomorrow
And that's today
And it's as thin as the line
That separates memories from dreams
So when walking that fine line of reality
One can only fall one way

Though there are those of us
Who dangle from that line
In an attempt to swing the wrong way

What fools we are
For embellishing in bedtime stories
Meant to uphold the fantasies of children
When we could be building upon our desires
Meant to uphold the visions of men

Being

New face old pain
It all remains the same
Unless the structure of the
Telescope has changed

So tell me is it enough to simply be?
Or shall I decree
To know a much better state of being wherein I am an absentee
Of myself that knows no glee?

Shall I follow that uncharted path
Where unverified lines are reminiscent of a banshee's silhouette?
Depossession is eminent yet still I allow this crossover to occur
This foreign trek where I've dismissed refined boundaries

In an attempt to continue this treasure hunt
But first I'm forced to confront
The lies that are at the brunt
Of this cold front

Clarification

Allow me to reintroduce myself
My name is not *Flower*
I was not planted here
To be pollinated

Yet you insist on trying to plant yourself
In between my roots
Claiming its only natural
To go all in on this
Raw from the start

But my last name is not *Field*
And this is not a game
Or a way for you to raise points

So don't get our roles twisted
I'm not the effect to your cause
You are not the interior to my exterior
I'm not your mirror

And you definitely are not my muse

Neither are you the water to my ship
Yet you insist on trying
To navigate me to places I do not care to go

I am not the beneficiary for your emotions

I am what you are not
Which is why we will never be

Time

I.
Drowning in the structured abyss
Beneath the lowly bayou's murky gates
Lies the low resolution dreams
Ill formatted by the depths of procrastination

The key to the encryption
Is historic like circular layers
It's all relative to this pandemic
Where minds are becoming acquired

Like prisoners to circumstances
They are screwed by the elements within the system

II.
All because Time…
She is a dictator
While Karma is a lustful harlot
Paying homage to all
Seeking to give everyone a bit of her time
So she lies in wait with the rustic bones
That decorate her lair

Autobiography: Your Story

I wish you were a character in my story
Under the control
Of my pen
My muse

I'd make you the doubled minded protagonist
Searching endlessly for the antagonist that
Hinders the development of your success

Then I'd grant you undeserved mercy by writing
In your turning point epiphany so you'd finally come
To understand the villain
Is the reflection that stares back at you

The villain is the shadow you can't
Get rid of
Because the sun only takes breaks
It always comes back

So you can only run from yourself for so long until I run
Out of pages or ink and even then
I'll leave your story open
With a cliffhanger
At each end because I'm far from done with you

So yes you would be your own series
I would give you hard lessons
In the form of loss and pain
Because experience is the only teacher
You seem to pay any semblance of heed to

I'd give you subplots to resolve
Let you attempt to reach the itch
Yet never get far

Too scared to overcome a few obstacles
To get the gold medal
You'll settle for the bronze, maybe silver
So you'll cautiously hold back

Then you'd continually curse the fate
That is trying desperately to bless you
So at the end of it all
You'll merely be another lost person
Who never made it to hero status

Perception

I.
A tree falls in a forest of absence and
Only the deaf can hear its collapse

The trees of our inner forest
Are like a synopsis
No one really wants to embark on the actual story
So we settle for the cliff notes version

There aren't enough masks
To cover the lifeless trees
Where evidence of neglect
Is not easily ignored

II.
I've fallen in between the seams
Of what seems to be the thinning extremes
As I continue to wait for dreams
To become more than mere themes
For the life that screams
To be more than what it seems

I've tried and I can't bribe
This old heart of mines to circumscribe
My own pride whose features
Mirror that of the great continental divide

A Soldier of Tears

Tear drops travel slower than the
Raindrops that let loose
From God's heaven
Yet I deduct
A tear is a tyrant in its own right
Leaving footprints in its path
For more soldiers to follow
They circle these red orbs
Before they separate into two army brigades

No one is safe as they hide deep in the trenches
Ready to launch their assault on unsuspecting lands
As many try to fight back the burn
The unshakeable foreshadowing
Of dueling with enemies once thought to be found
Only in cascaded reflections

Yet eventually
We all succumb to its forces
Like a body that ages

It is only a matter of time
Before we are caught off guard
By a soldier of tears

Blank Pages

I've gone through different stages
Yet these pages
Are still as blank as this ceiling
I suppose my muse must still be healing
From the last bleed out
Because there's no doubt
That a literary artery was ripped open
I'm still dizzy from the last time I let this pen
Gain so much free will
I told my mind to sit in the back seat that this wasn't a drill
I needed that release
So I could achieve some sort of peace
I'm so tired of silent poetics so I told my heart to go back and continue
        its hibernation
Till I'm through with this migration
Because I'm heading somewhere
But this compressed air
Has delayed my itinerary
So I'm forced to reroute my literary
Agenda yet and still something's got to give
Because my soul begins to live
In between the blank pages
And a full pen that's where I get my wages
My recompense for working in this field
But it's not enough that I can yield
Words that will make people stand still
No I need to know that my crop went deep down into your will
To stimulate and infect your psyche so you'll end up needing some of
        these blank pages
To get you through the stages
For when your muse decides to visit your confessional

True Story

I'm stuck
I can't wind backwards or speed forward
I'm stuck in a reality full of actualities
I choose to unobjectively ignore

My past is written in permanent ink
And replays like a taunt rhythmic anthem in my mind

I'd be a liar if I said each rerun didn't hurt

The benedictions I tried to ignore
And pass off as subtle fractions of darkness
Were really fragments of reality attempting to shed some light
On the ignorance I tried to make a security
Yet I completely overlooked the risk of that said security

So what's wrong?
Standing on off balance hindrances
Left pieces of me fractured
With no attempt of recovery measurable or in sight
Meaning the modern me is suffering from
The separation of the traditional

Yet and still…

I wake up from these dreams
Feeling like I've been drowning in streams
Of complexities because I haven't been able
To solve for the missing variable
Somewhere along the line
I missed the defining sign
So now I'm staring out at a field of trees
And I can't separate the X from the Y which leaves me with unease
As I run through the forest and
Enter the circus filled with familiar blank faces that have spanned
The scope of my mental land
And at this point I'm getting tired of doing nothing with firsthand
Warnings because my decoder has been breached
By the worms that have leached
Into my soul

Leaving me shamelessly touchy as I fight for control
Of the strangers that appear
To have trespassed into my mental territory

The Nature of Birds

Fall stayed true to His nature
And although I tried to stay true to mines,
When the time came to fly south
I found the standard deviation
Unhinged and unabridged.

It obstructed my view,
So I found myself
North of others expectations.
So they couldn't see me and I couldn't see them
Is this the nature of a white bird
Whose soul is as black as the ink that stains this paper?

How many feathers must I pluck
To leave as bread crumbs
To help me return
Back to where it all started,
Before I was kicked out of the flock
Before I was lied to and told,
"It'll be okay come and fly with us."

I don't even recognize me anymore.
Much less this old flight pattern my instincts are taking me on

Did I ever know where I was headed?
Have I been following flight patterns embedded in my literary DNA
Or have I gone rouge
While straying from paths
That did little to sate my desires for growth?

Endangered Species

The display; the accuracy of simulation
Has left me perched upon the fork in the road
With primitive aspirations combating against
What should not be a rare find

Stooping down I join the march
Down the yellow brick road
Paved with good intentions
Trying to avoid the nearside attractions

Still a detour is a detour
I should have left that man alone
Then again my heart was cloaked with it's own intentions
Separate and hidden from my mind's eye

Then I ended up in the valley of broken dreams

Somewhere beneath a broken rainbow
Where the wishing well stands covered in ash
An aching soul yearns for the rest
Where hope is most fruitful

The place where sleep causes one to awake
And separate from
Socialistic mentalities
That hinders ones ability to regulate and breathe
While subsisting in this valley of
Broken promises and jagged dreams

Wrong Direction

Counter

-ing against the rhythm of the wind
I've become so confined
in this flight which is far from the peace of mind
journey that I had in mind
but I didn't fly downwind
so I fell behind

Clock

-ing my thoughts in overtime
yet it must be a crime
to separate the tick from the tock with such a sublime
form of mind because I can't get a penny for my thoughts yet
alone a dime
I must be in the wrong zone for time
yet dare I say that I'm

Wise

in my own reprise because I must confess
this repetition has got me on a blind mission to oppress
that which does transgress against my success
even though it is evident I should revise my coordinates to
better address
that which motivates the resistance that tends to press
against my transition but in either direction time is such a
limited edition commodity where I can't digress from this
game of chess

When the Heart & Mind Converse

"Well no proper reference to you is needed
You know well who you are.

I sit up at the top for a reason
Yet you refuse to adhere to my rule.

My reason is not without understanding
Yet you continue to seethe at my alleged lack of compassion.

This separation isn't going to work.
You're to act as beta to my alpha

Not go out and form your own.

Your concessions are weakening.
A feat I prize of my own benefactor."

"Yes I know well who I am
You should be grateful for the balance I provide.

I'm settled in middle for a reason
Yet you don't even ask for my help in the middle of a season.

You may be filled with sense but I
Am what heads morality,

The compassion of character.
Left with only you there is nothing.

Don't ignore the hand that
Keeps you steady lest
You're ready for a nice long fall."

Control Freak

We need to break these chains
Of condemnation that keep us in bondage

We put our dreams
Up for sentencing and
Some of them even get
The death penalty

We have no space for
Redemption but we give plenty
Of room for judgment
And condemnation

We make ourselves
The judge and executioner
Of our own fate
Because we can't see past our need for control

We wreck God's plan
For us then we
Bicker and complain
When He cleans up
Our mess because we
Don't have the capacity
To see past the pain
And at the breakthrough
That change causes

En Route

Good medicine is always bitter

So let me explain
How I became a phantom
Reflecting ghostly lines
Because all of these skeletons aren't all mines
Some wanted me to be the beneficiary
For their own emotions
Yet when pen crashes into paper
Pandora's box has been opened
And the truth flows like a flood

People struggle to wade through it all
Some drown – never making it close to the surface

In any event
I will continue to navigate
Through these waters of confession
Because conviction is my compass
And salvation is my destination

Fed Up

I.
What's on my heart?
It's hard to tell at times
With the weight
Of other people taking up space

I need to erase it all
Before I am caught up in other people's disgrace

II.
I don't need a piece of your mind
Because I'm quite satisfied with my own

I could put you in a verse and
Cry my tears through my stanzas
I could let the readers experience my pain
Like they're siphoning my vein
But I'm sick and tired of it all

You're a parasitic being
That I've spent far too much time entertaining

I'm sick and tired what you call
Normal relations when really it's
A power trip and I'm being dragged along
For this sadistic ride you call a relationship
While you try to strip me of power to fill your own void

You've set me up as your peddle
That you press on when
You're trying to get somewhere

So what's really on my mind?

The weight of my heart
Is temperamental
The time is coming when the dam will someday break and
Parasites like you will drown
Because boundaries will become a memory
Like lands washed away

With no warning

It will happen because you constantly
Hold onto your own insecurity
Like it's a life vest

In reality it is
The dead weight that will do you in
And turn you into the memory
That will fade away into nothing

Swimming

Arriving upon the shore of revelation,
I take several breaths of dictation
so that I may avoid the damnation

that waits in the evening tide.
My exhales are complex, being denied
the simple right to divide

the grains of sand
that hold my soul up; and
yes they betray me on command,

washing away when the waves
of temptation kiss the graves
that have made slaves

of my transparent emotions.
But I have determined these notions
lead to thoughts of promotions.

So I graduate from a crawl
and approach this walk with small
and even steps because above all

I must be watchful and maintain
my relationship with evolution and abstain
from the intimate relations that leave me in vain.

So I digress
and confess
that which does address

the real meat, flesh, and bones
of the problems that end me up in these zones
where I'm left standing at the altar of my mind throwing stones.

Where I also wonder who altered the creations
of my desires which affected the generations
of actions and thoughts bred into the foundations

of my character? So here I am pulling weeds
that I didn't plant with my seeds,
watch me now because the tide always recedes

causing erosion to flush across the face
of my disgrace
so now I'm left with perfect grace

I've got no choice but to hold on tight
to the revelations that navigate my fight
because I'm tired of reliving the genesis of my life in second sight.

How many apples shall be bitten
before it is a given
that experience can't be unwritten?

Drip drip, that's all I hear
as the ink begins to disappear.
Nevertheless, I refuse to stay here

Because I am no longer grounded.
I am an alumnus of experience where I've founded
the Philosophy of Manifestation without being astounded.

I was built for this experience
and I'm speaking in all forms of the tense
it was no pretense

That this journey landed me here
on this new frontier.
I'm in the middle of an epiphany that's making it all too clear.

You will find
tomorrow's bullet in yesterday's gun barrel if you fall behind
and leave today in the backseat, so bear in mind

you can't condition time
to flow on your own rhyme and I'm
inclined to admit it's a crime

of passion to rub two abstract
thoughts together and think that
you won't become an accessory after the fact.

Then again, your heart, your heart screams no justice no peace.
So you engage your common sense in this tug of war where you refuse
     to cease
Because you don't care to be right you really don't want to be the only
     one wronged and without peace.

So I can't help but disclose
how relativity will have levy blows
because Consequence is the only one
that has time on its side to tax and impose.

My Muse Speaks

Who am I but a subconscious feign

I'm your hooked on phonics
Because I need you learn…

I am the one that
Can make you cry
A river to float away
From the nightmares
You need me to lyrically profess
So you can literally digress
From the fears that oppress
Your awaiting success

I am biased by nature
Yet still opened ended at the seams
You made me that way
So don't put me down

You are my sire
They make you angry and
I will deconstruct them
With any feat of my choosing

I am universal
And multi-purposed

I am a delinquent of normalcy
Yet innocently so

I am a rule breaker
I will not be censured
So don't read me

My cries and screams
Are the dreams
You've tried to live
Within the seams of reality

So you carry me around like a blanket

For security

I am a route
To the self-discovery you fear
The reason you keep
Writing on the same topics, tears, and fears

I mate constantly
Birthing expressions you'd
Wish were stillborn

I am diverse
Yet I can pinpoint you out
My words
My love
My disgust
My anger
My…

Its directed
At you
Not at you
At someone like you
At someone far from you

My voices vary in strength like a storm
You never know which category
I'm going to be in
It depends on what
Mindset I want to leave you in

I am hypnotic
My verses are
Seductive and clairvoyant

I am your weapon
Your drug
Your aphrodisiac
Your security

Together we analyze you and solve for x
Only to inject you with carefully rethought
Chemical compounds so you get high

Off your own product
Till it brings us to tears
So we need to slow it all down
Then start all over again

You go to war with me
You build prisons and homes
All the while ignoring
The thinning line in between

You give me life
Yet try to rob me of it easily
Forgetting my immortality
You started me
Yet it is you who lives on through me

Your legacy is evident in my effect

I'm created the moment I mate with paper

I am this
I am that
Most importantly
Never forget
I am that which made you this
So when you reminisce
On the facts
Of what brought you to your own start
Remember

I am poetry
I am you
I am not you
I am your lover
Which means
I am your enemy

I am your subconscious feign

Moderation Denied

I will not be moderated
Check out my litography
I am a purebred poet
I was not converted nor is this feat
Some religious practice
Like the Christians
That are only Christians on Sunday and
The occasional Wednesday
This is not a habit

I am not a writer three days out of the week
I was born with this love in my veins
That's why I bleed the way I do
My muse has cut my literary artery
The words won't stop

I will not be moderated
I am an artist
Which means I'm uncut
Unscripted
Unrehearsed
I stay deep
And complex
But never compressed
Because when I lyrically express
With finesse my distress
That hinders my successes
I'm only trying to remove you without stress
To a mentality that produces a better state of blessed success

The Night Shift

The cars past by
The wind blows
Life continues
It doesn't pause
Not even while I
Write whimsical verses
Hoping to find…something

I can't find the moon to gaze upon
Nor stars to wish upon
There's been a change

Too many unnatural lights liter the sky
I would if I could
Clean the sky of this sanitation and
Post new constellations
For the empty dreamers to fill up on

Where do I give the most attention?
To the dream killers
That stole the stars
And left us with a sky as dark as our hearts?

Or do I focus on the thief who hid the moon and
Tried to leave us with a counterfeit version that didn't last?

Although we still have the sun
Many of us don't come to ourselves until
Darkness falls so while the sun sets
Like a curtain over the horizon
So shall we rise as warriors working the night shift

The Epiphany of Grace

Poetic Interlude: Intro to 2014 Edens

Lately my poems have come off as a rant
But only because I'm trying to shed these words
Off my heart
So I can rid myself of this heartburn
That eats away at my lining

I feel stuck
And these struggles
Cause friction throughout my verses
So yes, I go from high to low points
Corrupting the status quo
So no this isn't a romance
Piece unless we talking
About the chivalry
That died a long time ago back
When the world handed me dead roses
As time stood in the back
Like a reversed Cyrano de Bergerac
Feeding us both lines of temptation

So give me a minute
As I continue to digress

These brick confessions
Being laid are building roads
And bridges because hey
I'm trying to get somewhere
And I'm hoping my foundation is solid
I don't want to fall and drown in the
River of lost manifestations

But first I got to get this compass straight
Because if I'm not careful I'll be moving
Forward into the same old sin
Wondering how I fell so artificially within
Realities that never even begin

Now let me get back to my rant

2014 Edens

The old tree is gone and
These new roots they
Won't hold
And no one cares to solve
The problem because
We're all too busy
Condemning one another
Trying to build our own
Individual Edens that
We refuse to share

Yet let someone trespass
And eat from our tree
And then it all goes to hell
I can tell
We're too busy drunk on
Opportunity to care

Jumping simultaneously
From the role of Adam
Who turned a blind eye
To Eve who was deceived
To the Snake who
Was the deceiver

Unsure of which of the three
Was the original sin
We can't remain in the same skin
For more than one sin
As we self-consciously
Tell ourselves that a character
Switch will redeem us
Not realizing that all three are with sin

Man these 2014 Edens…
Last I checked
You can't sow dead seeds
And expect it to be enough to feed
The dreams that you need to succeed

So why are we so eager to do it all backwards?
Don't we get that the
Mathematics is off?
We can't get 10 from 2+2
Yet we continually sow little
And expect a tenfold harvest
And oh yea the harvest comes
However it's nothing but weeds
So then we feel the self-entitled need
To curse every other sower especially
The ones with no weeds
Because yes look at how fruitful their harvest is
They must have done something corrupt
To get their seeds
To take perfect root

And all of this happens
Because we fail to realize and
Accept that whatever we feed will grow
Hope and faith lay dead
Because it's the things
We lust after that
We incorrectly seek to feed
Not understanding that lust
Is an insatiable beast
That will eventually devour us
As we give what we never even had

I'm not done…

Because let someone invite
Us into their Eden
Then we don't know how to act
We're too concerned with
What they have and
What we have not
To even care
That someone is trying to do right

Which gets me to my next point…
Where do we get off with this deity mentality?
No one else wants to address it
Who do we think we are

Passing judgment and
Delivering life sentences
Through broken promises and
Mistreated hearts all because
We've decided they're not worthy
Yet and still we expect someone
To overlook our lack of goodwill
Like we're too high up the spiritual hill
When really the only hill
We are high up on is our own
Molded crap

We can't be judge and victim
At the same time yet
We believe we do it so well as we
Try to turn our individual
Edens into modern day prisons for profit

So really we don't care about penance
We don't care about forgiveness
Or second chances either
We care about benefits
Because we only seek to satisfy
A need a for a 'lil while
That's why nobody's patient anymore
Ain't nobody trying to leave behind
Roots for no one anymore
Seed, time, harvest – what?
Those are foreign concepts to even
The holiest of us these days

I'm not preaching
I'm merely beseeching
You all to abandon and impeach
These individual Edens
That we've somehow fooled
Ourselves into believing
Are actually healthy for us

If we're struggling so hard
To build a fruitful home
Then why can't we simply
Evict ourselves and move on

Go reside in His home

I mean He already sent
A skilled Carpenter to do the work
He provided blueprints
And detailed aspects of the design
Yet we're tossing it all to the side
Saying it's too hard without
Even reading the plan

So Eden lies built
The original Eden
Not these 2014
Counterfeit versions

Its multi-purposed and universal
It's our infirmary and
Our battle station
It's got an impenetrable fortress
So it can never be taken from us
It's a teaching ground
Where sinners become students
Students become instructors and
Instructors become intercessors
Evangelists, apostles, warriors and the like

Its home

In case I went to deep
For some of you all
Let me bring this whole point
To the surface

We're wasting time
Trying to go by our
Our own design
When really there is only
One carpenter
One construction manager
And these Edens
That we keep trying to build
They're not even
A close impression

Of the real the thing
And they never even last
And frankly I don't want
To be homeless anymore

Dreaming Tree

Spare me a leaf
If not a fruit
That I may
If not permanently
Fancy a tarry
By the presence of
Absentee moments
Of bliss that
Always seem to pass
Me by during the harsh
Seasons that permit
No rest to the weary
Soul that longs for the
Touch that confidence brings
Due to perfect peace

Come
Shed upon me
That which is meant to separate
That I may be caught up
In your travel of time
That I may become
Apart of it's journey
Before it touches ground
The place where
The cycle rebounds

Dreaming Tree
Why won't you let me
Carve out a spot in
Between your roots
So I may bask
In the radiance
That befalls you
That I may grow
In harmony with your roots
Because I only want to be
Like a tree
Firmly planted with guaranty
I'll be tended to by the same streams

That nurture you, Dreaming Tree

The Perfect Chair

I.
Carved from the True Vine
Sculpted by the Carpenter
With four legs: faith, grace, the anointing, and the blessing
A strong lean back infused with mercy and favor
Painted, coded red with promise
Primed with divine love

Lean on me

II.
Pause…
Close your eyes
Exhale before you inhale
Bask in the freshness of the paint
The strength that upholds you
While the world tramples on your shoulders
Notice how you never hit the floor

Now get up

Your weight is balanced

He will never drop you
So long as you rest in Him
Because He fell lower than any man could

Return to Self

I. The Truth
I'm standing at the start line
I feel like I'm at the beginning -

Like the first part of a sentence
I haven't even begun to dive in
And swim through the language of thought and expression

- I'm standing outside the woods
And even though the wilderness is dense
With the promise of trials and tribulations
I can see Him in the center

He tells me to come His way
Where the path is worn
Where His footsteps once walked
It's not my imagination
And this is far from a drill
I'm too committed to quit
And some would call me crazy
For boldly trekking across the devil's playground
Yet this armor is not for decoration
Nor is it some fashion statement
To suit my character's appearance

II. The Prophesy
I see Him there
I see us here
Trudging through hell's climate
Closing in
To get to the center of it all
The climax of a thought backed by a vision
That teleports us across the time of pain
So we're flying faster than the speed of a broken heart
Because the prodigal child has returned

I see us picking back up our roles of being
Keepers for our sisters and brothers
Allowing them to lean on us
As we walk together, faster

Instead of at arms
Against one another

Some will run
With holy tongues
Weapons out and posed
Holding down the front line and backing the rear

Some will limp
At a determine pace
Perfectly suited with experience at spotting the enemy

Some will even crawl
Carrying scars and all

Regardless the state or condition
We continue towards the center of balance
Because the closer we get
The more vivid the vision becomes

The other part of ourselves
The main part stands
Waiting for us to return
Because we spent the prime of time
On the other side
Where we've lied, cried, and tried
To do it on our own
Acting like we didn't need a 66 book edition
To serve as our map
Yet even after getting lost
And finding ourselves

How sweet is the completed thought
That the pathway to His throne
Is still open
No specific hours
No fine print
Simply that the kingdom is ours to inherit
If we choose to accept it

Heads or Tails

I found myself in a tirade
Between the man on my left
And the man on my right

The man on my left
Passed me an apple martini.
Said, "It's on the house."

Before I could take a sip
The man on my right
Interjected and said,
"Have you checked the menu
For what else is offered?"

I didn't try and hide the look
That passed across my face.
The look that asked a million
Questions that all surmised to one,
"What are you doing in a place like
This?"

He let a custom smile cross his face,
As if he was used to the question.
He responded, "My child, I am everywhere,
More so than the air you breathe."

"His will is his own," said the man on my left,
"Let him choose for himself."

"A man may choose for himself but let him be aware
That all paths lead to only two places."

He ignored the loose tongued man and continued
Speaking, "What does it profit an artist to have tools
If he knows not how to use them correctly?"

Warrior Mentality

You call me crazy
Because my temperance
Remains moderate

What's really insane though
Are your antics
The consistency of which
Defines the root insanity
Of the hater mentality you hone

I am not a mountain to crumble
I am the tree firmly planted
With vines that sprout forth from
His Fountain of Life

I'm not blind
I see you
I see you trying to uproot me and
Separate me from my promise
I see you
I see you trying to steal my prosperity

You think I'm not fighting back
Because I haven't warred with your flesh
But on the spiritual level
I'm a warrior
I know how to pray and fast
And fall so deep into His grace
That my name is no more
There is only Him

Which in His terms
Is like taking a double edged sword to your heart
So no I don't place curses
This isn't a matter of witchcraft

Which is why in the end
His end
I'm happy for an eternity
Unlike you who's solely trying

To survive through a season
Like a thief in the night

Go ahead and steal
So my Father can find you
And make you return it sevenfold
I'll be waiting right here
Letting patience have its perfect work

The Death of Sin

The devil is a liar
I am a child of the most high God
I am not too far gone

Nor is my Lord and Savior still on the cross
He is seated on the right hand of the Father
Interceding on my behalf

So the cross I bare
Every cross that I bare
Every burden that weighs

Every trouble that lingers on my spirit
Comes pre-covered in His blood
Because He said I shall not bare beyond my limit
I was born ready for this
Born ready to grow into this manifestation

The devil is a liar
My Jehovah Jireh blessed my name
With His sacrifice and left me with a blood inheritance to claim

So when I abase my knees
And let the tears fall
Vertical to the nigh of the hour
I'm rich with blessings
Because I've zeroed out
Only to be spiritually upgraded

Yet this devil would have me think
My sins are my chains
No

Christ
My Christ bore the strifes
Of my sins in exchange for
The burdens of a shepherd
A state I gladly proclaim

A Poet's Prayer

Lord,
I can't do this on my own
I've had so many steep hills to overcome
And rocky valleys to go through

Then I refocus my focus
And remember that the steps
Behind me aren't my own

You carried me through the valley
Like a child
You are my light
And my way
Moving me forward
Is no issue for you
You easily brought me up the mountain
And sustained me through my journey in the valley

So Jesus I need you
I'm a flower
No I'm a seed
You are my fountain of life
Without you I'm unevolved
And underdeveloped

* * *

Lord,
Please guide the path of my pen
Let the flow of my tongue
Be in tempo with your will
So a soul will see me for the microphone
That I am
One that amplifies the voice of the Father

Under Construction

Deep within the trenches of my mind
I tend to find valleys of discarded confessions
Formed by varying levels of hysterical storms
That tore through my already fragile resolve

I'm standing amongst the debris
Trying to find out where to go from here
Trying to find something solid to hold onto
Trying to find a semblance of something familiar
Because familiarity is comforting
But I've got nothing
Nothing except a landfill of strongholds and mentalities
I'm struggling to overcome

It's a daily struggle ascertaining
How things got to the level they did
Then again I didn't pay erosion any heed
Until it was the final hour and
I was left with nothing other than me and the isms
That landed me here at this point
I'm corroded
And I've got no one to blame outside of myself
For entertaining notions conceived
From fixed thoughts
That didn't allow for much latitude

That was then
And now its time to rebuild
Because it wasn't until I was broken
That this purge could begin
It wasn't until I was broken that
I was able to see and acknowledge
That my directions were all wrong
Because I wasn't using the proper plans
For building a sound foundation

In retrospect I can boldly say
I am not a depository
For defunct emotions and mentalities
I am a temple

Undergoing renovation
Because God is not through with me yet
God is not finished with me
I am continually being restored for the better
Because Jesus
His birth
Death
Resurrection
And ascension
Was my down payment
I've been brought and paid for
And my slate has been wiped clean
It was His plan all along from the beginning

I am a temple
We are temples
Museums filled with testimonies
That attest to His great love

I mean He could have left us alone in our sin
But His love for us was so intense
That He created a new way out

And detours or diversions didn't alter His overall goal
To ensure that we would be adopted into His family
By and through Jesus

I mean what happened in the Garden of Eden
Didn't change His plans

So what can I...we say to all this?
No matter where we are in our renovation
Be convinced and assured
That whatever good work God started in us
He will continue perfecting it
And He will bring it to completion in due season

Epilogue

Explicit Confessions

I have become a vigilante of myself while
Trying to avenge these…
These wounds, these tears, and these screams
I have put aside my peaceful reputation
So I can accurately
Peel skins off and
Expose hearts
Then hold them in my hand
Only to whisper and
Embed these sordid memories of mine
I mark them with the scarlet letter "T" for thievery
For puncturing and stealing time
For gambling this precious commodity away
And investing it into the souls of other professional two tongued
         thieves

I have become a delinquent of normalcy
The current state of affairs
Because when it comes to my heart…my mind
This is not a democracy
You do not get a vote

These confessions have left me pixilated
All people see are the stranded pieces of me
Not the increases I've made
The fears I've abandoned to become something greater
So now I'm a bandit
Traversing these pages
Stealing moments of time from prying eyes
Leaving footprints across these verses

And yes I'm going all in bare this time
No pretty rhymes no dressy meters
No sweetness to help you digest it

Pandora's Box

At times my words are hard to digest
Because many are not mentally prepared
To handle the grown up portions that I deliver

I'm not theatrical
So here I am with this copasetic nature

Now I could feed you 'lil verses
Talk about the sky and the sun
How they relate to my love

Or I could talk about my dreams
And how they metaphorically
Sit on the landing strip
Waiting for the skies to clear

My words are deep like the ocean floor though
You have to go beneath the surface meaning
To understand the point I'm getting at

Because I'm not elementary in my approach
This is natural skill
That I perfect through experience

I don't merely speak these words
I bleed them
So when I'm at this mic
I'm committing suicide
But don't get it twisted
I'm not a martyr
I need to let some things die

Someone needs to open up Pandora's box
I can't be the only one who wants to be free
I can't be the only one who's tired of keeping this all inside

So when ink touches paper
When my voice penetrates this mic
I gain my freedom
Because it's the equivalent of me going to war

My verses are the 'lil soldiers
Standing up at the front line
Working around the clock

So every time I pause…
I'm reloading
Adding more soldiers to the battle and
More warriors for the cause

I fight because we are all kings and queens
I fight because someone along the line
Told you that you didn't deserve to be a king
That you didn't deserve to be a queen
So I fight for awareness
I fight for truth
Because I'm here to tell you
You are not defined
By your circumstances
You are not defined by your past
And you are most definitely are not defined by your pain

You are defined by your responses
You current action
In this moment of time
So speak and be heard
I don't mean speak with your tongue
I mean speak with your way of life
It's time we mastered this language
The art of being

People will not listen to our words
Until we make them more than just words
People will not listen until our words
Become the preface, the prologue for change
The precursor for actions to follow
So let your measures, the method in which you live be the translator
Because they may close their eyes
And block their ears
But they can't evade the effects
Because we are the cause
We will not stop

So come and open up pandora's box with me

Add your soldiers with my soldiers
Verses upon verses
Freedom poem after freedom poem

Trust me when I say
It feels so good to be free
And get rid of everything that prevented me from being me

I'm trying to set the atmosphere here
A solid foundation for us to build upon
Because I'm always vertical in my approach
My direction is always upward so
Don't ever look for me to be in the same spot twice
Because as long as I breathe…I evolve
As long as I evolve I change
As long as I change I am always
Shedding these layers
Because bare is beautiful
Because I am not ashamed of me
Because I am not ashamed of these scars
That represent that I lived
Because I…have lived
I have loved
I have cried
I have grieved
And not necessarily in that order

Yet people say the truth hurts
That it's more than we can bear
That it festers worse than a lie because a lie brings comfort
But the truth…
So many of us aren't grown up enough to deal with the reality
That the truth isn't here to make us feel good

The truth is a journey
In and of itself
One that can navigate us
To the better part of ourselves

Yet so many of us are afraid
Of being stretched
Across different seasons
Then we wonder

Why faith believers are considered
An endangered species today
Why the name-it and claim-it crew
Seems to be hiding underground
Nowhere to be found

So this leaves us with a blind spot
Where we can't see the chain reaction
This generational curse is causing
As we've ceased trying to breed
Kingdom minded warriors

All of this happens
Because we fail to step up and
Be the change we want to see

We find it easier to point fingers
Because the blame game
Means we don't have to step up
And own whatever it is that we keep
Hidden away in this dark little box

Trust me I've seen it
I've seen the wars
I've seen men
Struggle between two minds
Slowly eradicating any sign of design

Wars

I've seen wars
Where men chase the dreams of fools
In lands made up of anecdotes unlived

I've heard the screams souls choose as
Forgotten legends close their eyes to nightmares
Not their own only to awaken to realities that do not fit

I've seen wars
I've seen defeat
I've seen the white flag raised
Before the battle was even initiated

Call me crazed but
I've seen defeat start as early as the womb
Because we've stopped trying to breed warriors
Nobody is 'Kingdom' minded anymore
Nobody is 'Kingdom' minded anymore

I've seen wars
I've seen defeat
I've seen struggles

I've seen the platforms shake
Like two tectonic plates
You wouldn't see it at first
Until you looked at the whole picture
You couldn't see it at first
Because the drift was so continental
You will need a map
To navigate through the fault lines
Created by the chains of pride
Wrapped way too tight

And this inactivity is only adding
Links to the chain
Till its gets tighter and tighter
And harder and harder till you can't breathe
Till these dreams suffocate and die
And become casualties of the wars

That take place within our own mind
Don't become a casualty of war

The Breakthrough

I take steps forward
In a backwards direction
Only to realize too late my misstep
In this game of chess called life.

I've been focusing on the
Wrong moves, I left my valuable
Pieces unguarded but in
The final hour, backed against
The wall only the hunter and
The hunted remain and I don't
Know on which side I fall
When the opponent is myself.

I don't know which side I fall on
When the opponent is this little
Girl screaming with a muted voice
Asking to be visible and invisible at
The same time.

I don't know if I'm the hunter or the hunted
When the opponent,
My opponent,
Is this vengeful woman trading
Forgiveness for vendettas
Because she's tired of having dirt kicked in her face.

I don't know which side I fall
When the opponent is battling me
On fault lines waiting for our tectonic tendencies
To rub together and cause this quake
That's happening right now.

See…no one knows that
At times I feel like
I can't even speak
Because too many of them
Are screaming and fighting
For their chance at the podium

And the lines…they blur.
It gets confusing
Because my worst enemy
Isn't the devil
But the reflection that
Whispers in my ear
Late in the hour of my days.
So no one but me hears
What the enemy within is saying.

So I don't know if I should let
These emotional convicts roam free
From this prison
But I do know that
It is all falling apart.
I feel like there is a revolt
That's about to take place
And I don't know which Alice will survive
Because this…
What's about to happen
Is unprecedented.

And yes I…I am guilty right from the start
Guilty of standing on the sidelines
Thinking I could be neutral,
When in reality there's no such
Thing as impartial territory
Because a double mind is a terrible thing.

Let me fast forward.
I've been trying to get these
Words off me
But they're stuck on me
Like a second skin now.
I feel raw and exposed,
Naked in an unfamiliar way.
I'm foreign to my own self,
Which causes me to become an enemy of myself.
Not me
But the me I'm trying to get rid of.
The me that's up in the middle of the night
Tossing and turning
With no more tears left to shed.

The me that's tripping over her own heart.
So I wear this reckless ambition like a makeup
Because it's the only war paint that I have at this point.

I can't walk a straight line in this fight against myself
Because this,
I've got to get my hands dirty in this.
This is not a polite war
Where similes and metaphors
Create images that make you
Warm and tingly.
This is a blood bath where literary arteries are ripped open
And indecent exposure of the self is at its highest.
This is an old fashioned war
Where I eat, sleep, and fight on this battlefield
Because this
This is a purge.

There are no shortcuts to manifestation
And it can't be earned like most people think
It must be brought and paid for.

And I know in the beginning
It didn't sound like
This poem was going to
Be about Christ
But it is because
I've come to the conclusion
That it all keeps coming back to Him.
There is nothing I could have done
To earn not even a small measure of His Grace or hope.
He is the one that balanced my soul out.
That one brought me into right standing with the Father.
It's because of Him I don't have to fight this or any other battle alone.

This is good because I can't trust myself
So I need a mediator for my soul
And I'm not ashamed to admit
That it's a daily struggle.

Emotions can become the devil's playground,

But this…this is my breakthrough

God saw my end from the beginning.
He knows His thoughts are to give me an expected end and
I've come to the realization that
I can rest in the peace that confidence brings
Because I got my confidence from my faith, which gave me access to
   hope.
That same hope that developed from the
Experience of being patient
Through each trial I've gone through.

So this is my breakthrough.
He is my advocate,
My Beginning and my End.
He is my Rock,
My Savior,
My El Shaddai, and
My Elohim.
He is my vine.

He is the Carpenter of my path.
He is my breakthrough
And this herein is my epiphany

About the Poet

Alice Saunders currently lives in Tampa, Florida. She is the author of two poetry books: *Affirmation of Addiction* and *The Forgotten Lyrics*. Her poems have appeared in the *OW Newsletter* and *BLACKBERRY: a magazine*. She is also an editor at TL Publishing Group LLC. Her forthcoming titles include *Pandora's Box* and *Melissa's Story*.

She can be emailed at asaunders@torridliterature.com.

Website: http://lyricaltempest.com

Facebook: http://facebook.com/poetalicesaunders

Twitter: http://twitter.com/lyricaltempest